Christina Rossetti

Passion & Devotion

First published in Great Britain by Brockhampton Press,
a member of the Hodder Headline Group,
20 Bloomsbury Street, London WC1B 3QA

ISBN 1 86019 387 0

Created and produced by Flame Tree Publishing,
part of The Foundry Creative Media Company Limited,
The Long House, Antrobus Road, Chiswick, London W4 5HY

Special thanks to
Kate Brown and Kelley Doak for their work on this series

Printed and bound in U.A.E.

Christina Rossetti

Passion & Devotion

Written and Compiled by
K. E. SULLIVAN

Contents

Introduction

Christina Rossetti was an impassioned and prolific poet, ranking high in the pantheon of nineteenth-century English literature. Her talents are often understated, indeed, unrecognized in some quarters. From her published works shine gems of unquestionable merit, but her originality, the true breadth of her vision, is apparent mostly in the less popular works, in which she expresses an intense awareness of her culture, her womanhood, her religiosity and the vocabulary of loss. She simmers with unspent passion, exploring the depths of human emotion – in particular, renunciation and love – and expresses a preoccupation with death and loss, embroidered and fancified, but at the same time lucid and overwhelmingly inventive.

Her life was as dramatic as her finest work, and the considerable suffering she underwent throughout her career is reflected in her verse, which becomes progressively deep as her talents matured. She was born in London in 1830, the youngest of four children. Her father Gabriele Rossetti was an exile from Italy, and a Professor of Italian at King's College, London. He had a talent for pen and ink drawings and a flair for music, acting as librettist to the operatic theatre of San Carlo. The whole of Rossetti's family was imaginative and accomplished in the arts, pursuits encouraged by both parents. The household's conversation teemed with literary asides, poetic references and artistic analogies. It was a playhouse of the clever, eager and intelligent, and each family member had a role to play, clipping poetry into every conversation, quoting the finest literature. Her brothers were Dante Gabriel, a leading member of the Pre-Raphaelite Brotherhood, and an artist and poet himself, and William, a critic and civil servant, who went on to edit Christina's collected poems after her death.

Her sister Maria was a nun in one of the new Anglo-Catholic orders, and each family member had their own passions and obsessions. The children were brought up speaking and writing Italian and English, and Christina wrote poetry in both languages.

Christina was an intense child, precocious and invested with artistic sensibility from an early age. She was lively and mischievous as a girl, and then self-controlled and distantly polite as an adult. She took her art seriously, and had her first volume of poetry published at the age of seventeen, by her grandfather. The Rossetti household was lively, and often the meeting place for the Pre-Raphaelites, a group of painters who revolutionized the history of art. Christina became engaged to one of its members, James Collinson, but religious differences came between them, and when Collinson pledged his faith to Catholicism, she grandly renounced their union.

Christina was deeply and pedantically religious, which marked her poetry for most of her life. The English church was the focus of her enormous personal enthusiasms, and anything that threatened that bond was instantly rejected. She reeled with humanitarian principles and good intentions. She despaired of the plight of women in the Victorian age; she railed against indulgence in any form; she volunteered to nurse during the Crimean War under Florence Nightingale, but when that became an impossibility, she threw herself into the cause of the poor in London. Her life was a mission; her poetry an independent and intrepid bid for freedom.

Her work reflected her intense emotions. She longed for passionate love, and her despair at the break-up of her relationship with Collinson infiltrated her work for some time after the event. She shuddered at the prospect of sexual union, but longed for its release. She believed in the spirit as opposed to the body, and clearly believed on a non-sexual level that women could love other women as deeply as they could any man. Indeed, her unwittingly feminist approach to life was years before its time. She also wrote delicate children's poems, nonsense verse, and exquisite and expressive passages on the love of children and nature.

She loved flowers, and celebrated the changing seasons in most of her work. Her first great success was *Goblin Market and Other Poems*, published in 1862 and greeted with considerable critical attention. It was written in the form of a simple fairy tale, but with far more intricate images. Her wit and imagination are unparalleled in this selection of poems; in particular 'Goblin Market' is passionate and sensuous.

Her familial ties linked her with the Pre-Raphaelites, and she mistakenly became associated with their vision, although she did contribute poetry to their short-lived magazine *The Germ*, under a pseudonym. She sat as a model for a number of the Pre-Raphaelites; in particular, her brother's *The Girlhood of Mary Virgin*, which was painted under the supervision of his fellow Pre-Raphaelites, William Holman Hunt and Ford Madox Brown. Christina also modelled for the Virgin Mary in Rossetti's second Pre-Raphaelite painting, *Ecce Ancilla Domini*, or *The Anunciation*.

The circle of the Pre-Raphaelites embraced the cultural intelligentsia and literati of the day, and she was inspired by and tested wits with critics such as Edmund Gosse and John Ruskin, and richly creative minds like William Morris and Edward Burne-Jones. Her brother Dante Gabriel encouraged her to publish *Goblin Market*, and he also designed the volume's binding, title-page and frontispiece. He also provided the

binding and illustrations for Christina's second collection, *The Prince's Progress and Other Poems* (1866).

But in the end, her searching mind settled on religion as a fundamental focus, and she spent an increasing amount of time on her religious writings. Love of God transcended everything human, and she visibly mourned the Godlessness of the Victorian age. In 1866 she ended another relationship, this time with the writer Charles Cayley, because he announced that he no longer held religious beliefs, and she seemed to rejoice in her sacrifice for God. Her work had a bleak human message, but a rewarding and warming anticipation of death and the world that follows.

Her great spirit and devotion remained unfulfilled throughout her life, and although much of her focus is on her personal loss, she was a keen documenter of the Victorian world, and its inevitable contradictions.

Rossetti suffered from Graves' disease, and it is likely that it was this intractable condition which forced her to address her mortality, and to attempt an analysis of death. She was profoundly optimistic about death, and clearly drew great comfort from the beauty which she believed existed after life.

There is a rich vein of imagery running through her work, of which the eternal themes of life and death appear. She examines and queries the nature of love in many works, while others consider unrequited and frustrated love. Rossetti suffered from bad health for much of her life, leading her to be largely reclusive. Her introspection is eloquent, never self-indulgent, but she was considered and indeed is still considered to be melancholy. Rossetti was intensely private, insisting that each of her correspondents burned all of her letters, and she did the same to her own journals and papers.

She was well regarded by her contemporaries, including Lewis Carroll, with whom she corresponded for many years. He wrote that she was 'a genuine poet ... If only the Queen would consult *me* as to whom to make Poet-Laureate! I would say "for once, Madam, take a *lady*!"'

In 1866 she published *The Prince's Progress and Other Poems*, and nursery rhymes and works for children, among them *Sing-Song*, in 1872 and *Speaking Likenesses* in 1874. *A Pageant and Other Poems* was published in 1881. Her last volume of poetry, *Verses*, was published in 1893, a year before her death. Her later work was almost entirely devotional, and although she 'had no politics', according to her brother William, she threw herself into humanitarian causes, such as the anti-vivisection movement and the society for the protection of minors. Her last years were spent nursing her sick mother.

Christina Rossetti died of cancer in London on 19 December 1894, and she was buried at Highgate Cemetery, in the family plot. On the death of Tennyson in 1892, many regarded her as Britain's greatest living poet.

Author's Note

Christina Rossetti could easily be categorized as a Victorian visionary, with an intense preoccupation with death and sacrifice bordering on religious fanaticism. But underlying even her most popular work is a profoundly independent spirit, an astute and emotional exploration of her times, her religion, her sex and her sexuality. The following is a selection of her most engaging and revealing works, as well as those with an intrinsically different message that cannot fail to captivate.

Chronology

1830	Christina Georgina Rossetti born on 5 December.
1842	First poem written, entitled 'To My Mother'.
1845	Suffers a nervous breakdown.
1847	*Verses* published with money from her grandfather.
1848	First poems published in *Athenaeum*. Becomes engaged to James Collinson.
1850	Publishes poems in *The Germ*. Writes *Maude: A Story for Girls*. Severs engagement with James Collinson.
1854	Poems published in various anthologies.
1855	Meets group of women writers, including Bessie Raynor Parkes, and Adelaide Proctor.
1856	*The Lost Titian* published in *The Crayon*.
1859	Writes 'Goblin Market'.
1862	*Goblin Market and Other Poems* published; travels abroad to France.
1862	Joins portfolio society; contributes to religious anthologies.
1864	Begins Italian verse inspired by her new love Charles Cayley.
1865	Travels to Switzerland and Italy.
1866	*Poems* published. *The Prince's Progress and Other Poems* published.
1867	Moves to Bloomsbury.
1870	Begins to suffer from Graves' disease.
1871	Publication of *Sing-Song*, with illustrations by Arthur Hughes.
1875	New version of *Poems* published.
1879	Contributes to wide variety of devotional magazines and papers.
1881	*A Pageant and Other Poems* published. *Called to be Saints, the Minor Festivals devotionally studied* published.
1882	*Poems, New Series* published.
1883	*Letter and Spirit: Notes on the Commandments* published. Becomes involved in anti-vivisection campaign.
1892	*The Face of the Deep* published. Has surgery for cancer.
1894	Dies, 29 December. Buried in Highgate Cemetery.

Remember

REMEMBER ME when I am gone away,
Gone far away into the silent land;
When you can no more hold me by the hand,
Nor I half turn to go yet turning stay.
Remember me when no more day by day
You tell me of our future that you planned:
Only remember me; you understand
It will be late to counsel then or pray.
Yet if you should forget me for a while
And afterwards remember, do not grieve:
For if the darkness and corruption leave
A vestige of the thoughts that once I had,
Better by far you should forget and smile
Than that you should remember and be sad.

Cousin Kate

I WAS a cottage maiden
Hardened by sun and air,
Contented with my cottage mates,
Not mindful I was fair.
Why did a great lord find me out,
And praise my flaxen hair?
Why did a great lord find me out
To fill my heart with care?

He lured me to his palace home –
Woe's me for joy thereof –
To lead a shameless shameful life,
His plaything and his love.
He wore me like a silken knot,
He changed me like a glove;
So now I moan, an unclean thing,
Who might have been a dove.

O Lady Kate, my cousin Kate,
You grew more fair than I:
He saw you at your father's gate,
Chose you, and cast me by.
He watched your steps along the lane,
Your work among the rye;
He lifted you from mean estate
To sit with him on high.

Because you were so good and pure
He bound you with his ring:
The neighbours call you good and pure,
Call me an outcast thing.
Even so I sit and howl in dust,
You sit in gold and sing:
Now which of us has tenderer heart?
You had the stronger wing.

O cousin Kate, my love was true,
Your love was writ in sand:
If he had fooled not me but you
If you stood where I stand,
He'd not have won me with his love
Nor bought me with his land;
I would have spit into his face
And not have taken his hand.

Yet I've a gift you have not got,
And seem not like to get:
For all your clothes and wedding-ring
I've little doubt you fret.
My fair-haired son, my shame, my pride,
Cling closer, closer yet:
Your father would give lands for one
To wear his coronet.

Spring

FROST-LOCKED all the winter,
Seeds, and roots, and stones of fruits,
What shall make their sap ascend
That they may put forth shoots?
Tips of tender green,
Leaf, or blade, or sheath;
Telling of the hidden life
That breaks forth underneath,
Life nursed in its grave by Death.

Blows the thaw-wind pleasantly,
Drips the soaking rain,
By fits looks down the waking sun:
Young grass springs on the plain;
Young leaves clothe early hedgerow trees;
Seeds, and roots, and stones of fruits,
Swollen with sap put forth their shoots;
Curled-headed ferns sprout in the lane;
Birds sing and pair again.

There is no time like Spring,
When life's alive in everything,
Before new nestlings sing,
Before cleft swallows speed their journey back
Along the trackless track –
God guides their wing,
He spreads their table that they nothing lack, –
Before the daisy grows a common flower,
Before the sun has power
To scorch the world up in his noontide hour.

There is no time like Spring,
Like Spring that passes by:
There is no life like Spring-life born to die, –
Piercing the sod,
Clothing the uncouth clod,
Hatched in the nest,
Fledged on the windy bough,
Strong on the wing;
There is no time like Spring that passes by,
Now newly born, and now
Hastening to die.

A Triad

THREE SANG of love together: one with lips
Crimson, with cheeks and bosom in a glow,
Flushed to the yellow hair and finger-tips;
And one there sang who soft and smooth as snow
Bloomed like a tinted hyacinth at a show;
And one was blue with famine after love,
Who like a harpstring snapped rang harsh and low
The burden of what those were singing of.
One shamed herself in love; one temperately
Grew gross in soulless love, a sluggish wife;
One famished died for love. Thus two of three
Took death for love and won him after strife;
One droned in sweetness like a fattened bee:
All on the threshold, yet all short of life.

Song

OH ROSES for the flush of youth,
And laurel for the perfect prime;
But pluck an ivy branch for me
Grown old before my time.

Oh violets for the grave of youth,
And bay for those dead in their prime;
Give me the withered leaves I chose
Before in the old time.

An Apple Gathering

I PLUCKED pink blossoms from mine apple-tree
And wore them all that evening in my hair:
Then in due season when I went to see
I found no apples there.

With dangling basket all along the grass
As I had come I went the selfsame track:
My neighbours mocked me while they saw me pass
So empty-handed back.

Lilian and Lilias smiled in trudging by,
Their heaped-up basket teased me like a jeer;
Sweet-voiced they sang beneath the sunset sky,
Their mother's home was near.

Plump Gertrude passed me with her basket full,
A stronger hand than hers helped it along;
A voice talked with her through the shadows cool
More sweet to me than song.

Ah Willie, Willie, was my love less worth
Than apples with their green leaves piled above?
I counted rosiest apples on the earth
Of far less worth than love.

So once it was with me you stooped to talk
Laughing and listening in this very lane:
To think that by this way we used to walk
We shall not walk again!

I let my neighbours pass me, one and twos
And groups; the latest said the night grew chill,
And hastened: but I loitered, while the dews
Fell fast I loitered still.

Winter: My Secret

I TELL my secret? No indeed, not I:
Perhaps some day, who knows?
But not today; it froze, and blows, and snows,
And you're too furious: fie!
You want to hear it? well:
Only, my secret's mine, and I won't tell.

Or, after all, perhaps there's none:
Suppose there is no secret after all,
But only just my fun.
Today's a nipping day, a biting day;
In which one wants a shawl,
A veil, a cloak, and other wraps:
I cannot ope to every one who taps,
And let the draughts come whistling thro' my hall;
Come bounding and surrounding me,
Come buffeting, astounding me,
Nipping and clipping thro' my wraps and all.
I wear my mask for warmth: who ever shows
His nose to Russian snows
To be pecked at by every wind that blows?
You would not peck? I thank you for good will,
Believe, but leave that truth untested still.

Spring's an expansive time: yet I don't trust
March with its peck of dust,
Nor April with its rainbow-crowned brief showers,
Nor even May, whose flowers
One frost may wither thro' the sunless hours.

Perhaps some languid summer day,
When drowsy birds sing less and less,
And golden fruit is ripening to excess,
If there's not too much sun nor too much cloud,
And the warm wind is neither still nor loud,
Perhaps my secret I may say,
Or you may guess.

Echo

COME TO me in the silence of the night;
Come in the speaking silence of a dream:
Come with soft rounded cheeks and eyes as bright
As sunlight on a stream;
Come back in tears,
O memory, hope, love of finished years.

Oh dream how sweet, too sweet, too bitter sweet,
Whose wakening should have been in Paradise,
Where souls brimfull of love abide and meet;
Where thirsting longing eyes
Watch the slow door
That opening, letting in, lets out no more.

Yet come to me in dreams, that I may live
My very life again though cold in death:
Come back to me in dreams, that I may give
Pulse for pulse, breath for breath:
Speak low, lean low,
As long ago, my love, how long ago!

Song

WHEN I am dead, my dearest,
Sing no sad songs for me;
Plant thou no roses at my head,
Nor shady cypress tree:
Be the green grass above me
With showers and dewdrops wet;
And if thou wilt, remember,
And if thou wilt, forget.

I shall not see the shadows,
I shall not feel the rain;
I shall not hear the nightingale
Sing on, as if in pain:
And dreaming through the twilight
That doth not rise nor set,
Haply I may remember,
And haply may forget.

A Bruised Reed Shall He Not Break'

I WILL accept thy will to do and be,
Thy hatred and intolerance of sin,
Thy will at least to love, that burns within
And thirsteth after Me:
So will I render fruitful, blessing still,
The germs and small beginnings in thy heart,
Because thy will cleaves to the better part. –
Alas, I cannot will.

Dost not thou will, poor soul? Yet I receive
The inner unseen longings of the soul,
I guide them turnings towards Me; I control
And charm hearts till one they grieve:
If thou desire, it yet shall come to pass,
Though thou but wish indeed to choose My love;
For I have power in earth and heaven above. –
I cannot wish, alas!

What neither choose nor wish to choose? and yet
I still must strive to win thee and constrain:
For thee I hung upon the cross in pain,
How then can I forget?
If thou as yet dost neither love, nor hate,
Nor choose, nor wish, – resign thyself, be still
Till I infuse love, hatred, longing, will. –
I do not deprecate.

The First Spring Day

I WONDER if the sap is stirring yet,
If wintry birds are dreaming of a mate,
If frozen snowdrops feel as yet the sun
And crocus fires are kindling one by one:
Sing, robin, sing;
I still am sore in doubt concerning Spring.

I wonder if the springtide of this year
Will bring another Spring both lost and dear;
If heart and spirit will find out their Spring,
Or if the world alone will bud and sing:
Sing, hope, to me;
Sweet notes, my hope, soft notes for memory.

The sap will surely quicken soon or late,
The tardiest bird will twitter to a mate;
So Spring must dawn again with warmth and bloom,
Or in this world, or in the world to come:
Sing, voice of Spring,
'Till I too blossom and rejoice and sing.

A Better Resurrection

I HAVE no wit, no words, no tears;
  My heart within me like a stone
Is numbed too much for hopes or fears;
  Look right, look left, I dwell alone;
I lift mine eyes, but dimmed with grief
  No everlasting hills I see;
  My life is in the falling leaf:
    O Jesus, quicken me.

My life is like a faded leaf,
  My harvest dwindled to a husk;
Truly my life is void and brief
  And tedious in the barren dusk;
My life is like a frozen thing,
  No bud nor greenness can I see:
Yet rise it shall – the sap of Spring;
    O Jesus, rise in me.

My life is like a broken bowl,
  A broken bowl that cannot hold
One drop of water for my soul
  Or cordial in the searching cold;
Cast in the fire the perished thing,
  Melt and remould it, till it be
A royal cup for Him my King:
    O Jesus, drink of me.

The One Certainty

VANITY OF vanities, the Preacher saith,
All things are vanity. The eye and ear
Cannot be filled with what they see and hear.
Like early dew, or like the sudden breath
Of wind, or like the grass that withereth,
Is man, tossed to and fro by hope and fear:
So little joy hath he, so little cheer,
Till all things end in the long dust of death.
To-day is still the same as yesterday,
To-morrow also even as one of them;
And there is nothing new under the sun:
Until the ancient race of Time be run,
The old thorns shall grow out of the old stem,
And morning shall be cold and twilight grey.

The World

BY DAY she woos me, soft, exceeding fair:
But all night as the moon so changeth she;
Loathsome and foul with hideous leprosy
And subtle serpents gliding in her hair.
By day she woos me to the outer air,
Ripe fruit, sweet flowers, and full satiety:
But through the night, a beast she grins at me,
A very monster void of love and prayer.
By day she stands a lie: by night she stands
In all the naked horror of the truth
With pushing horns and clawed and clutching hands.
Is this a friend indeed; that I should sell
My soul to her, give her my life and youth,
Till my feet, cloven too, take hold on hell?

Dream-Love

YOUNG LOVE lies sleeping
In May-time of the year,
Among the lilies,
Lapped in the tender light:
White lambs come grazing,
White doves come building there;
And round about him
The May-bushes are white.

Soft moss the pillow
For oh, a softer cheek;
Broad leaves cast shadow
Upon the heavy eyes:
There winds and waters
Grow lulled and scarcely speak;
There twilight lingers
The longest in the skies.

Young Love lies dreaming;
But who shall tell the dream?
A perfect sunlight
On rustling forest tips;
Or perfect moonlight
Upon a rippling stream;
Or perfect silence,
Or song of cherished lips.

Burn odours round him
To fill the drowsy air;
Weave silent dances
Around him to and fro;
For oh, in waking
The sights are not so fair,
And song and silence
Are not like these below.

Young Love lies dreaming
Till summer days are gone, –
Dreaming and drowsing
Away to perfect sleep:
He sees the beauty
Sun hath not looked upon,
And tastes the fountain
Unutterably deep.

Him perfect music
Doth hush unto his rest,
And through the pauses
The perfect silence calms:
Oh, poor the voices
Of earth from east to west,
And poor earth's stillness
Between her stately palms.

Young love lies drowsing
Away to poppied death;
Cool shadows deepen
Across the sleeping face:
So fails the summer
With warm, delicious breath;
And what hath autumn
To give us in its place?

Draw close the curtains
Of branched evergreen;
Change cannot touch them
With fading fingers sere:
Here the first violets
Perhaps will bud unseen,
And a dove, may be,
Return to nestle here.

A Portrait

I

SHE GAVE up beauty in her tender youth,
Gave up all hope and joy and pleasant ways;
She covered up her eyes lest they should gaze
On vanity, and chose the bitter truth.
Harsh towards herself, towards others full of ruth,
Servant of servants, little known to praise,
Long prayers and fasts trenched on her nights and days:
She schooled herself to sights and sounds uncouth
That with the poor and stricken she might make
A home, until the least of all sufficed
Her wants; her own self learned she to forsake,
Counting all earthly gain but hurt and loss.
So with calm will she chose and bore the cross
And hated all for love of Jesus Christ.

II

They knelt in silent anguish by her bed,
And could not weep; but calmly there she lay.
All pain had left her; and the sun's last ray
Shone through upon her, warming into red
The shady curtains. In her heart she said:
'Heaven opens; I leave these and go away;
The Bridegroom calls, – shall the bride seek to stay?'
Then low upon her breast she bowed her head.
O lily flower, O gem of priceless worth,
O dove with patient voice and patient eyes,
O fruitful vine amid a land of dearth,
O maid replete with loving purities,
Thou bowedst down thy head with friends on earth
To raise it with the saints in Paradise.

Spring Quiet

GONE WERE but the Winter,
Come were but the Spring,
I would go to a covert
Where the birds sing;

Where in the white thorn
Singeth a thrush,
And a robin sings
In the holly-bush.

Full of fresh scents
Are the budding boughs
Arching high over
A cool green house:

Full of sweet scents,
And whispering air
Which sayeth softly:
'We spread no snare;

'Here dwell in safety,
Here dwell alone,
With a clear stream
And a mossy stone.

'Here the sun shineth
Most shadily;
Here is heard an echo
Of the far sea,
Though far off it be.'

A Dream

ONCE IN a dream (for once I dreamed of you)
We stood together in an open field;
Above our heads two swift-winged pigeons wheeled,
Sporting at ease and courting full in view.
When loftier still a broadening darkness flew,
Down-swooping, and a ravenous hawk revealed;
Too weak to fight, too fond to fly, they yield;
So farewell life and love and pleasures new.
Then as their plumes fell fluttering to the ground,
Their snow-white plumage flecked with crimson drops,
I wept, and thought I turned towards you to weep:
But you were gone; while rustling hedgerow tops
Bent in a wind which bore to me a sound
Of far-off piteous bleat of lambs and sheep.

Shall I Forget?

SHALL I forget on this side of the grave?
I promise nothing: you must wait and see
Patient and brave.
(O my soul, watch with him and he with me.)

Shall I forget in peace of Paradise?
I promise nothing: follow, friend, and see
Faithful and wise.
(O my soul, lead the way he walks with me.)

One Day

I WILL tell you when they met:
In the limpid days of Spring;
Elder boughs were budding yet,
Oaken boughs looked wintry still,
But primrose and veined violet
In the mossful turf were set,
While meeting birds made haste to sing
And build with right good will.

I will tell you when they parted:
When plenteous Autumn sheaves were brown,
Then they parted heavy-hearted;
The full rejoicing sun looked down
As grand as in the days before;
Only they had lost a crown;
Only to them those days of yore
Could come back nevermore.

When shall they meet? I cannot tell,
Indeed, when they shall meet again,
Except some day in Paradise:
For this they wait, one waits in pain.
Beyond the sea of death love lies
For ever, yesterday, to-day;
Angels shall ask them, 'Is it well?'
And they shall answer, 'Yea.'

Memory

I

I NURSED it in my bosom while it lived,
I hid it in my heart when it was dead;
In joy I sat alone, even so I grieved
Alone and nothing said.

I shut the door to face the naked truth,
I stood alone – I faced the truth alone,
Stripped bare of self-regard or forms or ruth
Till first and last were shown.

I took the perfect balances and weighed;
No shaking of my hand disturbed the poise;
Weighed, found it wanting: not a word I said,
But silent made my choice.

None know the choice I made; I make it still.
None know the choice I made and broke my heart,
Breaking mine idol: I have braced my will
Once, chosen for once my part.

I broke it at a blow, I laid it cold,
Crushed in my deep heart where it used to live.
My heart dies inch by inch; the time grows old,
Grows old in which I grieve.

II

I have a room whereinto no one enters
Save I myself alone:
There sits a blessed memory on a throne,
There my life centres.

While winter comes and goes – oh tedious comer! –
And while its nip-wind blows;
While bloom the bloodless lily and warm rose
Of lavish summer.

If any should force entrance he might see there
One buried yet not dead,
Before whose face I no more bow my head
Or bend my knee there;

But often in my worn life's autumn weather
I watch there with clear eyes,
And think how it will be in Paradise
When we're together.

L. E. L.

DOWNSTAIRS I laugh, I sport and jest with all:
But in my solitary room above
I turn my face in silence to the wall;
My heart is breaking for a little love.
Though winter frosts are done,
And birds pair every one,
And leaves peep out, for springtide is begun.

I feel no spring, while spring is wellnigh blown,
I find no nest, while nests are in the grove:
Woe's me for mine own heart that dwells alone,
My heart that breaketh for a little love.
While golden in the sun
Rivulets rise and run,
While lilies bud, for springtide is begun.

All love, are loved, save only I; their hearts
Beat warm with love and joy, beat full thereof:
They cannot guess, who play the pleasant parts,
My heart is breaking for a little love.
While beehives wake and whirr,
And rabbit thins his fur,
In living spring that sets the world astir.

I deck myself with silks and jewellery,
I plume myself like any mated dove:
They praise my rustling show, and never see
My heart is breaking for a little love.
While sprouts green lavender
With rosemary and myrrh,
For in quick spring the sap is all astir.

Perhaps some saints in glory guess the truth,
Perhaps some angels read it as they move,
And cry one to another full of ruth,
'Her heart is breaking for a little love.'
Though other things have birth,
And leap and sing for mirth,
When springtime wakes and clothes and feeds the earth.

Yet saith a saint: 'Take patience for thy scathe;'
Yet saith an angel: 'Wait, for thou shalt prove
True best is last, true life is born of death,
O thou, heart-broken for a little love.
Then love shall fill thy girth,
And love make fat thy dearth,
When new spring builds new heaven and clean new earth.'

What Would I Give?

WHAT WOULD I give for a heart of flesh
to warm me through,
Instead of this heart of stone
ice-cold whatever I do;
Hard and cold and small, of all hearts
the worst of all.

What would I give for words, if only
words would come;
But now in its misery my spirit
has fallen dumb:
Oh, merry friends, go your way, I have
never a word to say.

What would I give for tears, not smiles
but scalding tears,
To wash the black mark clean, and to
thaw the frost of years,
To wash the stain ingrain and to
make me clean again.

Life and Death

LIFE IS not sweet. One day it will be sweet
To shut our eyes and die:
Nor feel the wild flowers blow, nor birds dart by
With flitting butterfly,
Nor grass grow long above our heads and feet,
Nor hear the happy lark that soars sky high,
Nor sigh that spring is fleet and summer fleet,
Nor mark the waxing wheat,
Nor know who sits in our accustomed seat.

Life is not good. One day it will be good
To die, then live again;
To sleep meanwhile: so not to feel the wane
Of shrunk leaves dropping in the wood,
Nor hear the foamy lashing of the main,
Nor mark the blackened bean-fields, nor where stood
Rich ranks of golden grain
Only dead refuse stubble clothe the plain:
Asleep from risk, asleep from pain.

Vanity of Vanities

AH, WOE is me for pleasure that is vain,
Ah, woe is me for glory that is past:
Pleasure that bringeth sorrow at the last,
Glory that at the last bringeth no gain!
So saith the sinking heart; and so again
It shall say till the mighty angel-blast
Is blown, making the sun and moon aghast
And showering down the stars like sudden rain.
And evermore men shall go fearfully
Bending beneath their weight of heaviness;
And ancient men shall lie down wearily,
And strong men shall rise up in weariness;
Yea, even the young shall answer sighingly
Saying one to another: How vain it is!

The Lowest Place

GIVE me the lowest place: not that I dare
Ask for that lowest place, but Thou hast died
That I might live and share
Thy glory by Thy side

Give me the lowest place: or if for me
That lowest place too high, make one more low
Where I may sit and see
My God and love Thee so.

Beauty Is Vain

WHILE ROSES are so red,
While lilies are so white,
Shall a woman exalt her face
Because it gives delight?
She's not so sweet as a rose,
A lily's straighter than she,
And if she were as red or white
She'd be but one of three.

Whether she flush in love's summer
Or in its winter grow pale,
Whether she flaunt her beauty
Or hide it away in a veil,
Be she red or white,
And stand she erect or bowed,
Time will win the race he runs with her
And hide her away in a shroud.

Grown and Flown

I LOVED my love from green of Spring
Until sere Autumn's fall;
But now that leaves are withering
How should one love at all?
One heart's too small
For hunger, cold, love, everything.

I loved my love on sunny days
Until late Summer's wane;
But now that frost begins to glaze
How should one love again?
Nay, love and pain
Walk wide apart in diverse ways.

I loved my love – alas to see
That this should be, alas!
I thought that this could scarcely be,
Yet has it come to pass:
Sweet sweet love was,
Now bitter bitter grown to me.

Paradise: In a Dream

ONCE IN a dream I saw the flowers
That bud and bloom in Paradise;
More fair they are than waking eyes
Have seen in all this world of ours.
And faint the perfume-bearing rose,
And faint the lily on its stem,
And faint the perfect violet
Compared with them.

I heard the songs of Paradise:
Each bird sat singing in his place;
A tender song so full of grace
It soared like incense to the skies.
Each bird sat singing to his mate
Soft cooing notes among the trees:
The nightingale herself were cold
To such as these.

I saw the fourfold River flow,
And deep it was, with golden sand;
It flowed between a mossy land
With murmured music grave and low.
It hath refreshment for all thirst,
For fainting spirits strength and rest;
Earth holds not such a draught as this
From east to west.

The Tree of Life stood budding there,
Abundant with its twelvefold fruits;
Eternal sap sustains its roots,
Its shadowing branches fill the air.
Its leaves are healing for the world,
Its fruit the hungry world can feed,
Sweeter than honey to the taste
And balm indeed.

I saw the gate called Beautiful;
And looked, but scarce could look within;
I saw the golden streets begin,
And outskirts of the grassy pool.
Oh harps, oh crowns of plenteous stars,
Oh green palm branches many-leaved –
Eye hath not seen, nor ear hath heard,
Nor heart conceived.

I hope to see these things again,
But not as once in dreams by night;
To see them with my very sight,
And touch and handle and attain:
To have all Heaven beneath my feet
For narrow way that once they trod;
To have my part with all the saints,
And with my God.

Consider

CONSIDER
The lilies of the field whose bloom is brief: –
We are as they;
Like them we fade away,
As doth a leaf.

Consider
The sparrows of the air of small account:
Our God doth view
Whether they fall or mount, –
He guards us too.

Consider
The lilies that do neither spin nor toil,
Yet are most fair: –
What profits all this care
And all this coil?

Consider
The birds that have no barn nor harvest-weeks;
God give them food: –
Much more our Father seeks
To do us good.

A Smile and a Sigh

A SMILE because the nights are short!
And every morning brings such pleasure
Of sweet love-making, harmless sport:
Love, that makes and finds its treasure;
Love, treasure without measure.

A sigh because the days are long!
Long long these days that pass in sighing,
A burden saddens every song:
While time lags who should be flying,
We live who would be dying.

By the Sea

WHY DOES the sea moan evermore?
Shut out from heaven it makes its moan,
It frets against the boundary shore;
All earth's full rivers cannot fill
The sea, that drinking thirsteth still.

Sheer miracles of loveliness
Lie hid in its unlooked-on bed:
Anemones, salt, passionless,
Blow flower-like; just enough alive
To blow and multiply and thrive.

Shells quaint with curve, or spot, or spike,
Encrusted live things argus-eyed,
All fair alike, yet all unlike,
Are born without a pang, and die
Without a pang, and so pass by.

COLIN-LIBOUR-

Goblin Market
——— EXTRACT ———

MORNING and evening
Maids heard the goblins cry
'Come buy our orchard fruits,
Come buy, come buy:
Apples and quinces,
Lemons and oranges,
Plump unpecked cherries,
Melons and raspberries,
Bloom-down-cheeked peaches,
Swart-headed mulberries,
Wild free-born cranberries,
Crab-apples, dewberries,
Pine-apples, blackberries,
Apricots, strawberries; –
All ripe together
In summer weather, –
Morns that pass by,
Fair eves that fly;
Come buy, come buy:
Our grapes fresh from the vine,
Pomegranates full and fine,
Dates and sharp bullaces,
Rare pears and greengages,
Damsons and bilberries,
Taste them and try:
Currants and gooseberries,
Bright-fire-like barberries,
Figs to fill your mouth,
Citrons from the South,
Sweet to tongue and sound to eye;
Come buy, come buy.'

Sleeping at Last

SLEEPING AT last, the trouble and tumult over,
Sleeping at last, the struggle and horror past,
Cold and white, out of sight of friend and of lover,
Sleeping at last.

No more a tired heart downcast or overcast,
No more pangs that wring or shifting fears that hover,
Sleeping at last in a dreamless sleep locked fast.

Fast asleep. Singing birds in their leafy cover
Cannot wake her, nor shake her the gusty blast.
Under the purple thyme and the purple clover
Sleeping at last.

Venus's Looking-Glass

I MARKED where lovely Venus and her court
With song and dance and merry laugh went by;
Weightless, their wingless feet seemed made to fly,
Bound from the ground and in mid air to sport.
Left far behind I heard the dolphins snort,
Tracking their goddess with a wistful eye,
Around whose head white doves rose, wheeling high
Or low, and cooed after their tender sort.
All this I saw in Spring. Through Summer heat
I saw the lovely Queen of Love no more.
But when flushed Autumn through the woodlands went
I spied sweet Venus walk amid the wheat:
Whom seeing, every harvester gave o'er
His toil, and laughed and hoped and was content.

Love Lies Bleeding

LOVE THAT is dead and buried, yesterday
Out of his grave rose up before my face;
No recognition in his look, no trace
Of memory in his eyes dust-dimmed and grey.
While I, remembering, found no word to say,
But felt my quickened heart leap in its place;
Caught afterglow thrown back from long set days,
Caught echoes of all music passed away.
Was this indeed to meet? – I mind me yet
In youth we met when hope and love were quick,
We parted with hope dead, but love alive:
I mind me how we parted then heart sick,
Remembering, loving, hopeless, weak to strive: –
Was this to meet? Not so, we have not met.

Autumn Violets

KEEP LOVE for youth, and violets for the spring:
Or if these bloom when worn-out autumn grieves,
Let them, lie hid in double shade of leaves,
Their own, and others dropped down withering;
For violets suit when home birds build and sing,
Not when the outbound bird a passage cleaves;
Not with dry stubble of mown harvest sheaves,
But when the green world buds to blossoming.
Keep violets for the spring, and love for youth,
Love that should dwell with beauty, mirth, and hope
Or if a later sadder love be born,
Let this not look for grace beyond its scope,
But give itself, nor plead for answering truth –
A grateful Ruth tho' gleaning scanty corn.

'Consider the Lilies of the Field'

FLOWERS PREACH to us if we will hear: –
The rose saith in the dewy morn:
I am most fair;
Yet all my loveliness is born
Upon a thorn.
The poppy saith amid the corn:
Let but my scarlet head appear
And I am held in scorn;
Yet juice of subtle virtue lies
Within my cup of curious dyes.
The lilies say: Behold how we
Preach without words of purity.
The violets whisper from the shade
Which their own leaves have made:
Men scent our fragrance on the air,
Yet take no heed
Of humble lessons we would read.

But not alone the fairest flowers:
The merest grass
Along the roadside where we pass,
Lichen and moss and sturdy weed,
Tell of His love who sends the dew,
The rain and sunshine too,
To nourish one small seed.

Wife to Husband

—— EXTRACT ——

PARDON THE faults in me,
For the loves of years ago:
Good-bye.
I must drift across the sea,
I must sink into the snow,
I must die.

Long Barren

THOU WHO didst hang upon a barren tree,
My God for me;
Though I till now be barren, now at length,
Lord, give me strength
To bring forth fruit to Thee.

Thou who didst bear for me the crown of thorn,
Spitting and scorn;
Though I till now have put forth thorns, yet now
Strengthen me Thou
That better fruit be borne.

Thou Rose of Sharon, Cedar of broad roots
Vine of sweet fruits,
Thou Lily of the vale with fadeless leaf,
Of thousands Chief,
Feed Thou my feeble shoots.

After Communion

WHY SHOULD I call Thee Lord, Who art my God?
Why should I call Thee Friend, Who art my Love?
     Or King, Who art my very Spouse above?
     Or call Thy Sceptre on my heart Thy rod?
     Lo, now Thy banner over me is love,
     All heaven flies open to me at Thy nod:
     For thou hast lit Thy flame in me a clod,
     Made me a nest for dwelling of Thy Dove.
     What wilt Thou call me in our home above,
Who now hast called me friend? how will it be
When Thou for good wine settest forth the best?
Now Thou dost bid me come and sup with Thee,
Now Thou dost make me lean upon Thy breast:
     How will it be with me in time of love?

What's in a Name?

WHY HAS Spring one syllable less
Than any its fellow season?
There may be some other reason,
And I'm merely making a guess;
But surely it hoards such wealth
Of happiness, hope and health,
Sunshine and musical sound,
It may spare a foot from its name
Yet all the same
Superabound.

Soft-named Summer,
Most welcome comer,
Brings almost everything
Over which we dream or sing
Or sigh;
But then summer wends its way,
To-morrow, – to-day, –
Good-bye!

Autumn, – the slow name lingers,
While we likewise flag;
It silences many singers;
Its slow days drag,
Yet hasten at speed
To leave us in chilly need
For Winter to strip indeed.

In all-lack Winter,
Dull of sense and of sound,
We huddle and shiver
Beside our splinter
Of crackling pine,
Snow in sky and snow on ground.
Winter and cold
Can't last for ever!
To-day, to-morrow, the sun will shine;
When we are old,
But some still are young,
Singing the song
Which others have sung,
Ringing the bells
Which others have rung, —
Even so!
We ourselves, who else?
We ourselves long
Long ago.

One Sea-side Grave

UNMINDFUL of the roses,
Unmindful of the thorn,
A reaper tired reposes
Among his gathered corn:
So might I, till the morn!

Cold as the cold Decembers,
Past as the days that set,
While only one remembers
And all the rest forget, –
But one remembers yet.

A Chill

WHAT CAN lambkins do
All the keen night through?
Nestle by their woolly mother
The careful ewe.

What can nestlings do
In the nightly dew?
Sleep beneath their mother's wing
Till day breaks anew.

If in field or tree
There might only be
Such a warm soft sleeping-place
Found for me!

Johnny

——— EXTRACT ———

JOHNNY HAD a golden head
Like a golden mop in blow,
Right and left his curls would spread
In a glory and a glow,
And they framed his honest face
Like stray sunbeams out of place.

He and She

'SHOULD ONE of us remember,
And one of us forget,
I wish I knew what each will do –
But who can tell as yet?'

'Should one of us remember,
And one of us forget,
I promise you what I will do –
And I'm content to wait for you,
And not be sure as yet'.

Memento Mori

POOR the pleasure
Doled out by measure,
Sweet though it may be, while brief
As falling of the leaf;
Poor is pleasure
By weight and measure.
Sweet the sorrow
Which ends to-morrow;
Sharp though it be and sore,
It ends for evermore:
Zest of sorrow,
What ends to-morrow.

A Prodigal Son

DOES THAT lamp still burn in my Father's house,
  Which he kindled the night I went away?
  I turned once beneath the cedar boughs,
  And marked it gleam with a golden ray;
  Did he think to light me home some day?

Hungry here with the crunching swine,
  Hungry harvest have I to reap;
  In a dream I count my Father's kine,
  I hear the tinkling bells of his sheep,
  I watch his lambs that browse and leap.

There is plenty of bread at home,
  His servants have bread enough and to spare;
  The purple wine-fat froths with foam,
  Oil and spices make sweet the air,
  While I perish hungry and bare.

Rich and blessed those servants, rather
  Than I who see not my Father's face!
  I will arise and go to my Father: –
  'Fallen form sonship, beggared of grace,
  Grant me, Father, a servant's place.'

Golden Silences

THERE IS silence that saith, 'Ah me!'
There is silence that nothing saith;
One the silence of life forlorn
One the silence of death;
One is, and the other shall be.

One we know and have known for long,
One we know not, but we shall know,
All we who have ever been born;
Even so, be it so, –
There is silence, despite a song.

Sowing day is silent day,
Resting night is a silent night;
But whoso reaps the ripened corn
Shall shout in his delight,
While silences vanish away.

Death-watches

THE SPRING spreads one green lap of flowers
Which Autumn buries at the fall,
No chilling showers of Autumn hours
Can stay them or recall;
Winds sing a dirge, while earth lays out of sight
Her garment of delight.

The cloven East brings forth the sun,
The cloven West doth bury him
What time his gorgeous race is run
And all the world grows dim;
A funeral moon is lit in heaven's hollow,
And pale the star-lights follow.

'Behold the Man!'

SHALL CHRIST hang on the Cross, and we not look?
Heaven, earth and hell stood gazing at the first,
While Christ for long-cursed man was counted cursed;
Christ, God and Man, Whom God the Father strook
And shamed and sifted and one while forsook: –
Cry shame upon our bodies we have nursed
In sweets, our souls in pride, our spirits immersed
In wilfulness, our steps run all acrook.
Cry shame upon us! for He bore our shame
In agony, and we look on at ease
With neither hearts on flame nor cheeks on flame:
What hast thou, what have I, to do with peace?
Not to send peace but send a sword He came,
And fire and fasts and tearful night-watches.

Mary Magdalene and the Other Mary

OUR MASTER lies asleep and is at rest:
His Heart has ceased to bleed, His Eye to weep:
The sun ashamed has dropt down in the west:
Our Master lies asleep.

Now we are they who weep, and trembling keep
Vigil, with wrung heart in a sighing breast,
While slow time creeps, and slow the shadows creep.

Renew Thy youth, as eagle from the nest;
O Master, who hast sown, arise to reap: —
No cock-crow yet, no flush on eastern crest:
Our Master lies asleep.

Why?

LORD, IF I love Thee and Thou lovest me,
Why need I any more these toilsome days;
Why should I not run singing up Thy ways
Straight into heaven, to rest myself with Thee?
What need remains of death-pang yet to be,
If all my soul is quickened in Thy praise;
If all my heart loves Thee, what need the amaze,
Struggle and dimness of an agony? –
Bride whom I love, if thou too lovest Me,
Thou needs must choose My Likeness for thy dower:
So wilt thou toil in patience, and abide
Hungering and thirsting for that blessed hour
When I My Likeness shall behold in thee,
And thou therein shalt waken satisfied.

Index to First Lines

Notes on Illustrations

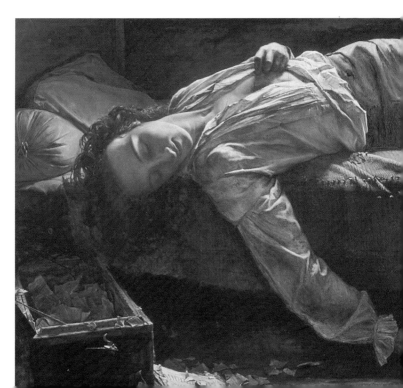

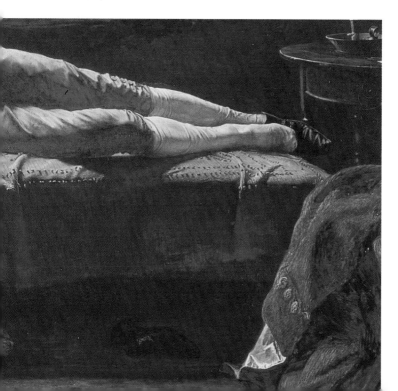